Sip it

Written by Zoë Clarke

Collins

Nip at a tip.

Tap in a tin.

Sit tins in it.

Tip tins in it.

Sit tins in it.

Tip tins in it.

Tip tip tip it.

Dip dip dip it.

Tip it. Tip it.

Sip it. Sip it.

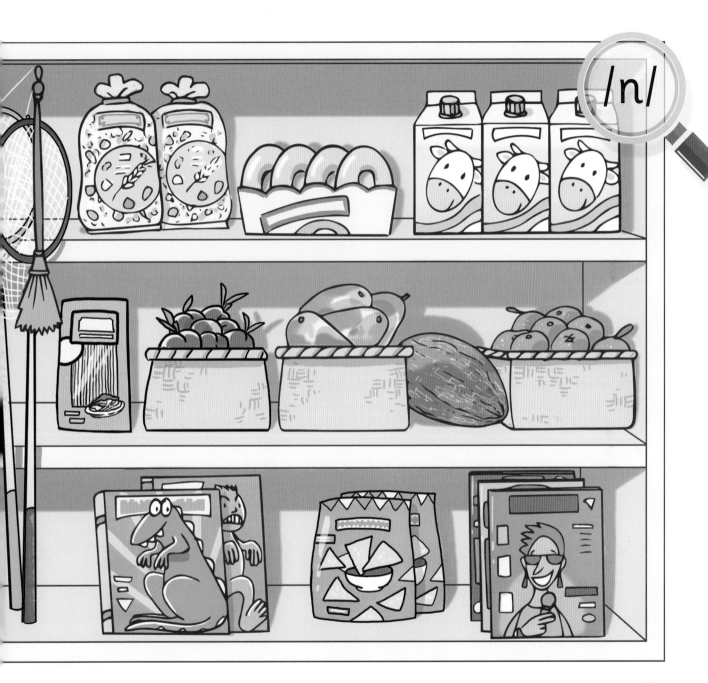

/n/

🐾 After reading 🐾

Letters and Sounds: Phase 2

Word count: 48

Focus phonemes: /s/ /a/ /t/ /p/ /i/ /n/ /d/

Curriculum links: Understanding the World: The World, People and Communities

Early learning goals: Listening and attention: listen attentively in a range of situations; Understanding: Answer 'how' and 'why' questions about experiences and in response to stories or events; Reading: read and understand simple sentences, use phonic knowledge to decode regular words and read them aloud accurately, read some common irregular words

Developing fluency

- Go back and read the chant to your child, using lots of expression.
- Make sure that your child follows as you read.
- Pause so they can join in and read with you.
- Say the whole chant together. You can make up some actions to go with the words.

Nip at a tip	Sit tins in it.	Tip tip tip it.
tip it tap it	Tip tins in it.	Dip dip dip it.
Tap in a tin.	Sit tins in it.	Tip it. Tip it.
tip it tap it	Tip tins in it.	Sip it. Sip it.

Phonic practise

- Say the word **dip**. Ask your child if they can sound out each of the letter sounds in the word, **dip**. 'd-i-p' and then blend them.
- Ask your child if they can find any words that start with the /t/ sound. (*tip, tap, tin*)
- Can your child find any words that end with the /t/ sound? (*sit, it*).
- Now look at the I spy sounds pages (14–15) together. Which words can your child find in the picture with the /n/ or /d/ sounds in them? (e.g. *newspapers, nuts, nets, nectarines, donkey, dog food, drink*)